Books by W. S. Merwin

TRAVELS

TRAVELS

POEMS BY

W. S. MERWIN

ALFRED A. KNOPF   NEW YORK

1996

THIS IS A BORZOI BOOK
PUBLISHED BY ALFRED A. KNOPF, INC.

Copyright © 1992 by W. S. Merwin

All rights reserved under International and Pan-American Copyright Conventions. Published in the United States by Alfred A. Knopf, Inc., New York, and simultaneously in Canada by Random House of Canada Limited, Toronto. Distributed by Random House, Inc., New York.

SOME OF THESE POEMS WERE ORIGINALLY PUBLISHED IN THE FOLLOWING PERIODICALS:

AMERICAN POETRY REVIEW: *Fulfilment, After Douglas, Lives of the Artists, A Short Nap On the Way, The Moment of Green, The Real World of Manuel Córdova*

ANTAEUS: *Manini, The Lost Camelia of the Bartrams, The Day Itself, Lunar Landscape*

THE ATLANTIC MONTHLY: *Cover Note, The Blind Seer of Ambon, Missing, So Far, Field Mushrooms*

FIELD: *Immortelles*

GRAND STREET: *The Hill of Evening, Barn, Rimbaud's Piano, Kites, Cinchona, Inheritance, The River, The Palms*

THE NATION: *Looking Up, One Story*

THE NEW YORK TIMES: *Last Morning at Punta Arena*

THE NEW YORKER: *Among Bells, The Morning Train, The Wars in New Jersey, Another Place, Rain Travel, On the Back of the Boarding Pass, On the Old Way, Left Open, Stone Village, Turning*

THE OHIO REVIEW: *For the Year*

POETRY: *Search Party, Panes, After the Spring, A Summer Night, Mirage*

Writing Lives was first published in *Leon Edel and Literary Art* (University of Michigan Press)

A Distance was first published in *A Garland for John Hollander*

Library of Congress Cataloging-in-Publication Data

Merwin, W. S. (William Stanley), 1927–
    Travels : poems / W.S. Merwin.—1st ed.
      p.   cm.
    ISBN 0–679–75277–3
    I. Title.
    PS3563.E75T7   1993
    811'.54—dc20
                              92–14917
                              CIP

Manufactured in the United States of America
Published January 17, 1993
Paperback Edition Published July 3, 1994
Second Printing, April 1996

For Margaret McElderry

CONTENTS

Contents

COVER NOTE

Hypocrite reader my
variant my almost
family we are so
few now it seems as though
we knew each other as
the words between us keep
assuming that we do
I hope I make sense to
you in the shimmer of
our days while the world we
cling to in common is

burning for I have not
the ancients' confidence
in the survival of
one track of syllables
nor in some ultimate
moment of insight that
supposedly will dawn
once and for all upon
a bright posterity
making clear only to
them what passes between

us now in a silence
on this side of the flames
so that from a distance
beyond appeal only
they of the future will
behold our true meaning
which eludes us as we
breathe reader beside your
timepiece do you believe
any such thing do the
children read what you do

when they read or can you
think the words will rise from
the page saying the same
things when they speak for us
no longer and then who
in the total city
will go on listening
to these syllables that
are ours and be able
still to hear moving through
them the last rustling of

paws in high grass the one
owl hunting along this
spared valley the tongues of
the free trees our uncaught
voices reader I do
not know that anyone
else is waiting for these
words that I hoped might seem
as though they had occurred
to you and you would take
them with you as your own

TRAVELS

Notes on some of the poems are on page 139.

THE BLIND SEER OF AMBON

I always knew that I came from
another language

and now even when I can no longer see
I continue to arrive at words

but the leaves
and the shells were already here
and my fingers finding them echo
the untold light and depth

I was betrayed into my true calling
and denied in my advancement
I may have seemed somewhat strange
caring in my own time for living things
with no value that we know
languages wash over them one wave at a time

when the houses fell
in the earthquake
I lost my wife
and my daughter
it all roared and stood still
falling
where they were in the daylight

I named for my wife a flower
as though I could name a flower
my wife dark and luminous
and not there

I lost the drawings of the flowers
in fire

I lost the studies
of the flowers
my first six books in the sea

then I saw that the flowers themselves
were gone
they were indeed gone
I saw
that my wife was gone
then I saw that my daughter was gone
afterward my eyes themselves were gone

one day I was looking
at infinite small creatures
on the bright sand
and the next day is this
hearing after music
so this is the way I see now

I take a shell in my hand
new to itself and to me
I feel the thinness the warmth and the cold
I listen to the water
which is the story welling up
I remember the colors and their lives
everything takes me by surprise
it is all awake in the darkness

MANINI

I Don Francisco de Paula Marin
saved the best for the lost pages
the light in the room where I was born
the first faces and what they said to me
late in the day I look southeast to the sea
over the green smoke of the world
where I have my garden

who did I leave behind at the beginning
nobody there would know me now
I was still a boy
when I sailed all the way to the rivers of ice
and saw the flat furs carried out of the forest
already far from their bodies
at night when the last eyes had gone from the fires
I heard wet bodies walking in the air
no longer knowing what they were looking for
even of their language I remember something
by day I watched the furs going to the islands
came the day when I left with the furs for the islands
it would always be said that I had killed my man

I still carry a sword
I wear my own uniform as the chiefs do
I remember the islands in the morning
clouds with blue shadows on the mountains
from the boat coming in I watched the women
watching us from under the trees
those days I met the first of my wives
we made the first of the children
I was led into the presence of the chief
whom the Europeans already called the king

we found what each of us
needed from the other
for me protection and for him
the tongues and meanings of foreigners
a readiness which he kept testing
a way with simples aand ailments
that I had come to along my way
I learned names for leaves that were new to me
and for ills that are everywhere the same

the king was the king but I was still a sailor
not done with my voyages
until I had been to both sides of the ocean
and other islands that rise from it
many as stars in the southern sky
I watched hands wherever there were hands
and eyes and mouths and I came to speak
the syllables for what they treasured
but sailed home again to my household and the king

since we have no furs here
he sent the men into the mountains
with axes for the fragrant sandalwood
it was carried out on their flayed backs
and sold for what they had never needed
all in the end for nothing and I directed it
with the wood a fragrance departed
that never came back to the mountains
all down the trails it clung to the raw backs
as the furs clung to the limbs of the fur-bearers
that fragrance had been youth itself and when it was gone
even I could not believe it had ever been ours

and when the king was dead and his gods were cast down
I saw the missionaries come
with their pewter eyes and their dank righteousness
yet I welcomed them
as my life had taught me to do
to my house under the trees by the harbor
where they stared with disgust
at the images of the faith of my childhood
at my wives at the petals our children
at the wine they were offered and the naked
grapes ripening outside in the sunlight
as we are told they once ripened in Canaan

I know these same guests will have me carried
by converts when my time comes
and will hail over me the winter of their words
it is true enough my spirit
would claim no place in their hereafter
having clung as I see now
like furs and fragrance to the long summer
that tastes of skin and running juice

I wanted the whole valley for a garden
and the fruits of all the earth growing there
I sent for olive and laurel endives and rosemary
the slopes above the stream nodded with oranges
lemons rolled among the red sugar cane
my vineyard girt about with pineapples
and bananas gave me two harvests a year
and I had herbs for healing since this is not heaven
as each day reminded me and I longed still for a place
like somewhere I thought I had come from

Manini

the wharf reaches farther and farther
into the harbor this year and the vessels
come laden from Canton and Guayaquil
I nurse the dying queens and the dropsical minister
I look with late astonishment at all my children
in the afternoon pearls from the inland sea
are brought to revolve one by one between my fingers
I hold each of them up to the day as I
have done for so long and there are the colors
once more and the veiled light I am looking for
warm in my touch again and still evading me

WRITING LIVES

for Leon Edel

Out of a life it is done
and without ever knowing
how things will turn out

or what a life is for that matter
any life at all
the leaf in the sunlight the voice in the day
the author in the words

and the invisible
words themselves
in whose lives we appear
and learn to speak
until what is said seems
to be almost everything
that can be known

one way with the words is to tell
the lives of others
using the distance as a lens

and another way
is when there is no distance
so that water
is looking at water

as when on a winter morning
as early as you can remember
while the plains were whitening
in the light before dawn
you saw your uncle—was it
your uncle?—reach
from the shadow and wash his face

to us it is clear
that if a single moment could be seen
complete it would disclose the whole

there is still that light in the water
before sunrise
the untold day

THE HILL OF EVENING

You will remember I think through the crowd
of events there how quietly the days
pass here on this hill where the two houses
most of the year seem to be the whole
of the inhabited world

at your last visit I was still living
in part of the big house above the steep
meadow with the old couple and their grown
children but we walked one afternoon
down the overgrown cart lane

through the woods and I showed you the smaller
empty house by the pasture where I live
now when I am here the windows facing
out from the trees onto the open hill
that falls away to the stream

we were talking of ambitions and age
and of change and I have come to think
of each age I should tell you as a season
always complete in itself as the days
here seem sometimes to be all

evening the hour when if you remember
we looked up from the lane in the first
twilight and saw the fine single stroke
of the new moon drifting across the valley
which is why I am writing to you

today a Sunday the day of visits
rare though they are on the hill but this morning
brought an old man on his way up the lane
to the big house who wanted to look in
here where he had known someone

in his youth and he sat till noon talking
of a time before I was born the encounters
in the lane the racing hearts the hayloads
the dancing all night in the valley and
walking back before daybreak

and then we went up the lane together
to the old woman's birthday party I
do not recall having seen so many
gathered there even at funerals and
today such triumphant celebration

as at a wedding flowers everywhere
long tables covered with white cloths under
the lime trees and the meal went on for hours
with the toasts the speeches and one by one
the old standing up in the waving

shadows of the leaves with a hush rising
around them and then from a distance their
voices approaching with moments out of
somewhere invisible to most of us
but still clear to some and indeed

what they still see around us and at last
the music of the roofer's accordion
and two violins with songs the old woman
asked for and a few of the middle-aged
got up and began the old dances

then the old were dancing and even the young
joined in laughing all circling to the one
time the tunes repeating over and over
nobody wanting them ever to stop
and the faces flushed the eyes wide

with surprise asking is it possible
is it happening and then it was over
they sat breathless or wandered off and when
I had said my farewells as formally
as though I lived far away

I started back down the lane for by then
it was already evening already
twilight and of course I was thinking again
of age and of what in each season seems
just out of reach just beyond what

is in front of us a kind of ghost
of what we see to which we offer up our days
and when you were here I could see that you hoped
I would have something to say to you about
all that and it was then that we

looked up to see the thin moon now this evening
there was no moon but in the long summer
grass to the right of the lane as I came
I saw a shining crescent a new sickle
bright as water and the blade

glittering with the dew and I stood there
as startled as the faces of the dancers
not knowing whose it could be how it had
come to be there what I was to do
with it now that I had seen it

leave it where it was to rust in the grass
and perhaps as I thought for a moment
to disappear to be really lost although
as you know no one steals anything here
and it must have been partly to see

whether it was really there that I reached down
and picked it up cool as the dripping grass
to carry home and lay on the table
here in front of me and tomorrow I must
try to find who it belongs to

BARN

In a cold May travelling alone across
stony uplands all afternoon the echoes
lengthening with the light and the tattered
crows exploding from their voices above
bare scrub oaks and jagged sloes each clutching
its fissured rock the wandering ruins
of pasture walls orchard enclosures rooms

and stairs of stone houses sinking into
thickets out of the late day like huddled sheep
still haunting shadows came the time to find
somewhere for the night and in that country
what had been built by hands to stand longest
outlasting the builders and their knowledge
was the barns set far apart from each other

emerging unpredictably from sides
of hollows as though from hiding but where
could creatures of such proportions have been
hidden on those swept barrens yet each
was nowhere to be seen until one came
by surprise upon a stone roof like a hill
half under trees a knuckled ridge a steep

starved slope descending to massive slabs
of eaves and on to buttresses shouldering
the low wall in which one square of night
a head taller than a man and an arm's length
wider than a man could reach an entry
framed in single hewn stones from which the doors
were long forgotten led in out of the dusk

Barn

in the vaulted ceiling there were stars already
and in the walls long portraits of lightning
coursing down to the ledges of empty
mangers but the wind was at once somewhere
from which a body had fallen and all
the hollow shadow echoed the absence
of breath the dumbness that had enfolded

at last the animals and the sighing
hay altogether with every voice that the
builders had harkened to and then the hushed
herders who had abandoned before the day
ended this dim hall this hill of stone
to which a foreigner would come at evening
and lie thinking of another country

RIMBAUD'S PIANO

Suddenly at twenty-one
with his poems already behind him
his manuscripts fed to the flames two years
since and his final hope
in the alchemy of the word buried
deep under the dust that chased his blown

soles through Europe and the fine
snows that spun into his slurring footsteps
in the passes southward to Italy
his shoes even then no
longer laced with lyre strings and his fingers
penniless once more then Italy

and its kind widow fading
backward into the darkness and hungers
of London Verlaine's retching and sobbing
the days of the Commune
his Paris dawns bursting for the first time
like poison promising through his blood

there he was back again at
Mother's after all at Mother's and not
even the farm at Roche with its crippled
barn where at least he could
have Hell to himself but the dank little
house on the crabbed street in Charleville

tight curtained like a series
of sickrooms the dimness reeking of walls
and waiting of camphor and vinegar
old bedding and the black
boards of Mother from which he kept turning
to the other door though outside it

there was nothing but Charleville
which he had left he thought and kept leaving
his pockets full of nothing but pages
now from dictionaries
Arabic Hindustani Greek Russian
he was learning them all and teaching

German to the landlord's son
with winter coming on trying to turn
some words into money into numbers
where the future lay but
there must be something to which the numbers
were still witness the harmony

that Pythagoras had called
music in whose continuo the light
burst into bodies knowing everywhere
the notes that were their way
those numbers that were their belonging and
Mother he told her I must have a

piano a piano
he said to her with her blue regard whose
husband had left her and the four children
both daughters sickly one
dying one son from the beginning good
for nothing and this other in whom

she had scrubbed brushed and buttoned
the last of her hopes for this world this one
who had been so good marching before her
to Mass and had won all
the prizes at school this one with the eyes
of ice who could have been anything

and instead had found nothing
better to do than run away like his
brother leaving her and the girls beside
the river telling them
that he was going for a book indeed
and taking the train for Paris with

no ticket letting her guess
what had happened to him with the Germans
advancing on Charleville and her breathless
from door to door searching
in cafes asking for him and all night
rummaging the street looking for him

not for the last time and he
already in the hands of the police
and bad company no wonder after
those books he had brought home
all his studies for nothing wandering
like a tramp with that other and now

a piano and Verlaine
to whom he wrote answered with that vomit
of piety perfected in prison
making it clear that this
long pretext for a loan was merely one
more trick to obtain money whereas

etcetera so he carved
a keyboard on the dining room table
for practising scales on while he listened
to his pupil's untuned
German and hearkened beyond them both
to the true sound until his mother

out of concern for the
furniture hired a piano which came
on a cart like part of a funeral
to be cursed through the door
as a camel and into its corner
thence to awaken the echoes of

Pythagoras as written
by Mademoiselle Charpentier in her
exercises for the pianoforte
borrowed from the Charleville
choirmaster her notations of those same
intervals that told the distances

among the stars wherefore
they sang stumbling over and over bruised
and shaky all that winter through the sour
rooms while his sister lay
dying while the doors were draped with mourning
before Christmas while the snow fell black

out of the death of the year
into the new the splintered ivory
far from its own vast sufferings sinking
into him daily its
claims so that by spring when he had acquired
a certain noisy proficiency

and the roads melted again
before him into visions of Russia
arches of Vienna faces of thieves
the waiting hands once more
of the police with somewhere beyond them
all a south and its peacock islands

its deserts and the battered
instrument was given up to become
a camel again patient on its own
pilgrimage to the end
of the elephants and its separate
molecules orbiting through unseen

stellar harmonies the drummed
notes of that winter continued to ring
in the heads that heard them they rose through
the oilcloth and the fringed
embroidery that hid the carved keyboard
they echoed the closing of the door

they spiralled after his steps
on the slave routes and slipped out of the first
words of letters from Africa useless
unwelcomed and unloved
without beginning like the trailing knock
of the artificial legs made for

his lost one but never used
heard by no others like the choir of eight
with five principal singers and twenty
orphans who bore candles
at his funeral and meaning nothing
else like the lives through which they sounded

AMONG BELLS

At the top of the dark
emerging from one more upward turn
on stones hollowed by feet so far ahead
that nothing of them would ever
be known

into the surprising
light still as glass around the green furred
hillsides of the bells as into a new
day fulfilling some forgotten
promise

lucid and with columns
beyond which bright clouds were travelling
almost within reach and the mountains rose
over the roofs of a foreign
city

a square with red tables
down there under dusty sycamores
Yugoslav flags kiosks posters loud in
Cyrillic across the flaking
facades

that contained the winding
streams of hats horses piled carts arms buses
making their way to and from the bevelled
lid of the train station with its
white clock

telling for each of them
a different age at the same time
even for the ancient belfry in which
the hour hovered as though nothing
that breathed

were living up under
its vaulted stone ceiling filled with beams
and the bronze domes of the bells but above
one of the blackened cornices
the wind

ruffled the shadowy
edges of a muted luster not
of stone a burnished swelling in the dust
some jewel of the air hiding
in air

quiet as a carving
a smooth wing of a swift so
still that nothing except wind seemed to move
in its feathers no flash of eye
betrayed

life in it the stiff quills
of course cold to the touch but then the
fine unseen softness above the spine warm
the hollow at the nape too and
the breast

yet all without motion
like a bundle with no weight at all
when lifted down the head drawn in eyes shut
feet curled tight upon nothing but
themselves

late in a cold summer
of dank grasses and dying forests
the taste of Lethe even in the mists
above the river and of burning
always

high in the air around
the towers above roofs among trees
dark by then with the knowledge of autumn
that bitterness climbing the air
from which

the feathers seemed to have
come so freshly no sign of blood no
visible injury the bill gleaming
like a chip of twilight the feet
perfect

the wings before they could
be seen to flash suddenly vanished
out of the cradling palms to reappear
trembling on the stone balustrade
one eye

for a moment glancing
back as a black planet after which
it was gone with a shriek into the long
afternoon light that touched the net
of wires

the waiting aerials
bare poles lines of laundry chimney flues
patched roofs pots of geraniums windows
standing open while in the streets
the same

hats legs and wagons were
moving toward unchanged destinations
and at the station trains were arriving
on time without a sound and just
leaving

SEARCH PARTY

By now I know most of the faces
that will appear beside me as
long as there are still images
I know at last what I would choose
the next time if there ever was
a time again I know the days
that open in the dark like this
I do not know where Maoli is

I know the summer surfaces
of bodies and the tips of voices
like stars out of their distances
and where the music turns to noise
I know the bargains in the news
rules whole languages formulas
wisdom that I will never use
I do not know where Maoli is

I know whatever one may lose
somebody will be there who says
what it will be all right to miss
and what is verging on excess
I know the shadows of the house
routes that lead out to no traces
many of his empty places
I do not know where Maoli is

You that see now with your own eyes
all that there is as you suppose
though I could stare through broken glass
and show you where the morning goes
though I could follow to their close
the sparks of an exploding species
and see where the world ends in ice
I would not know where Maoli is

MISSING

Last seen near the closing newstand
outside the cigar store angled
at that notorious corner
where some hasten past with eyes
downcast or with gaze clinging
to nothing beyond the propped
stacks of sooty rags settled
on headwaters of dark

rivers at the top of the steps
to the downtown subway while
some dressed for the breaks
in gleaming black revolve their
deliberate invitations
some circle menacing and one
who has been wrung through a long
life into garments with no size

will be delving whenever it is
through the piled cage of garbage
searching for anything all of them
backlit by store windows
arrayed with faded umbrellas
elderly luggage dust-filled
sunglasses portraits of foreign
beauties from other eras wreathed

in gold suggesting a good
smoke this hand suddenly
there thrust forth palm up out of what
had seemed to be nowhere one
more after so many but this
surprisingly clean and in
that light looking as though it
belonged to someone familiar

almost recognizable
and out of place there the eyes
in the bare youthful face filled
with terror disbelief tears
out of the mouth nothing while the hand
trembling from its recent launching
among those shadows kept floating
away from a figure

of height somewhat less than average
age perhaps thirty or
thirty-five hair blond cropped short clean
eyes no color at that hour but
no doubt blue cheeks pink and clean
body slight but not thin wearing
a short-sleeved striped jersey
clean his feet in white jogging shoes

beside him on a leash his
small part-shepherd bitch well fed brushed
answering to the name Bowama
looking up expecting kindness
standing on hind legs at the sound
of her name to look at his face
happy to be with him and sure
that everything would be all right

PAUL

Up the sea-dark avenue
at two in the morning a shadow
comes shouting oh
you mother-fucker I hate you Paul
echoes of feet and then
I hate you I hate you Paul

the old moon is sinking through
clouds beyond high wires and cornices
the buildings creak
drifting on the tunnelled hour the call
bounces ahead along
the street like a fleeing ball

there after each of the few
cars has passed over its words Paul you
can't get away
I hate you with my feet in the Paul
street like a bell I know
you are there you nowhere Paul

I am coming after you
whatever you do whatever you
think I hate you
across the street into the doors all
the way through the frozen
windows up against the wall

listen to me I hate who
you are nobody else will ever
hate you the way
I do I always hated you Paul
the whole time thinking you
could hold out on me that small

invisible you but to
me listen there was nothing to you
I was onto
you fooling with me your slick tricks all
the while and I hate you
where you are everywhere Paul

I go on hating you through
the roar of the Paul subway the red
lights at the Paul
cross streets out of sight into the Paul
night that cannot be touched
and does not turn when I call

KITES

No one who did not have to
would stay in the heaving sepia
roar of the unlit depot hour
after hour as some do
shoved and elbowed in the hot
breath of a rotting mouth yet there are
women sitting on the cement floor
suckling babies and among

the shoes that are never still
down under the shouting and the thin
flickering of hands burning and
going out there are some
of all ages sleeping as they
wait to be overtaken and to
wake at their time and find themselves housed
in white boards on the bench

of the almost empty car
while outside the gray windows that face
into the cooked air of the city
they see close beside them
a new life with afternoon light
shimmering as though reflected from
water along the dusty walls and
on green weeds glittering

then already before the
walls begin to slip there are the square
pieces of color in the tan
sky skipping and soaring
those small kites with invisible strings
that will beckon as guides for
so much of the way reappearing
over the first vacant

rubble fields and the children
running with raised arms in the distance
then over the scalped hill with its
family of shadows
breathless against the sky looking up
to the spirits dancing far
above them that must feel like their own
appearing to need no

wind at all to be leaping
high above the white layer of smoke
that covers what is called the world
and to be waiting with
others above the dark trees beyond
a ringing bridge a river
too slow to be real a path along
the low bank through the shade

and they keep turning to look
down from their clearer place onto roofs
at the rims of green terraces
braided houses a man
by himself planting while the hens on
the dump smoking at the end
of a lane search among waving ghosts
of translucent plastic

and all the way to the hills
and into the mountains the kites will be
watching from their own element
as long as the light lasts
neither living as the living know
of it nor dead with the dead
and neither leaving nor promising
the hands that hope for them

A DISTANCE

I would not go to such a place
the young overweight doctor said
raising his needle to the fluorescent hour
a boy running on the grass path
between flat pieces of light is holding
high something he has caught
that leaps and flashes in the sudden

late brightness of its life scarcely
do the ducks along the bank step
out of the way and the man standing
bent almost to the surface in
the water does not look up
from his reflection in which he is placing
one green stalk a straight thin strand

of smoke is rising from a white
pile on the far side of the water
by the hand-plastered tombs where hens
bow in the shade of banana leaves
beyond them tile roofs palm crowns bamboo walls
clusters of white columns what
are you holding above your head child

where are you taking it what does it know

THE MORNING TRAIN

In the same way that the sea
becomes something else the moment we
are on it with its horizon all around
us and its weight
bearing us up so a journey seems not
to be one as long as we are

travelling but instead we
are awake sitting still at a bare
window that is familiar to us but not
in truth ours as
we know and facing us there is a line
of socks hanging in the sunlight

over a patch of onions
blue in their summer luminous rows
of carrots the youth of lettuces to be
glimpsed once only
dahlias facing along a white painted
picket fence beside a plum tree

at the side of a station
like so many into which the green
revolving woods pointing fields brief moments of
rivers bridges
clusters of roofs again and again have
turned slowing first and repeating

their one gesture of approach
with a different name out of the place
of names a clock on which the hour changes
but not of course
the day arrangements of figures staring
through the last stages of waiting

only there is nothing on
the platform now but the morning light
the old gray door into the station is
standing open
in a silence through which the minute hand
overhead can be heard falling

while a hen is talking to
herself beyond the fence and why are
we not moving what are we waiting for now
only the hum
in our ears continuing to tell us
that we have been travelling since

whatever day it was that
city with its tower and there was
the night with its iron ceilings echoing
couplings through the
shunted hours in the all night restaurant
between trains then the socks begin

to slip away on their line
the garden swings softly behind its
fence and in a few hours when we think we are
almost home at
last we will look up through the pane across
a stony field plowed since we left

rusting at noon and the same
flowers will be leaning on the south
wall of the house from which we have watched the trains
pass and we will
see clearly as we rush by all of its
empty windows filled with the sea

FULFILMENT

The way the smoke
blew away and the tread of vagrant
stars through the nights of autumn
white wings out of season and raw calls when
the ice broke these were
predictions and at times we knew what they
told us was approaching

but what could we
do to prevent a day from ending
or a winter from finding
us how could we stop a wind with no home
from sliding into
our sleep or keep our parents from death
or ourselves from leaving

though we said to
the animals look how we taste you
with reverence the gut for
continuing in warmth through all the
snows the heart to flare
high in us look how you give yourselves
to us and we eat of

you only our
small days may you be many and we
here like the unceasing
water only the last foretelling was
already the touch
among us that we could not yet see
it seized us without our

Fulfilment

knowing that it
was near us it approached in shapes most
familiar to us it breathed
out of the animals and we grew faint
and believed they had
betrayed us then the strangers appeared with
their new ways of killing

which they exchanged
for skins of animals we thought were
no longer our family
so we pursued those swift spirits like fire
until they had turned
to smoke blown away and the world where we
had known them had turned to smoke

blowing away
then elders children old friends beside
fires had walked into a night
few of us drifted through a time of year
we had never seen
without leaves or color and we could hear
rendings and echoes that seemed

to cry out of
us as we were departing the world
of the strangers but we were
learning at last that we were still a word
of the prophecy
though some of us lived to see it begin
to happen finally

nobody will
remember you they said *nobody*
will believe you ever stood
in the daylight no one will wish to know
what we did to you
only in our words will anyone hear
what we choose to say of you

and it is true
they are what they forget and they make
records of all they are not
they turn themselves into a sky of smoke
before the next wind
wherever they go they race farther from
home in a night that opens

without end when
summer is done and the last flocks have
vanished and from the sleepless
cold of the unremembered river that
one voice keeps rising
to be heard once once only once but there
is nobody listening

THE LOST CAMELIA OF
THE BARTRAMS

All day
the father said we rode
through swamps
seeing tupelo

cypress standing in deep water
and on higher ground palmettos
mingling with pine
deer

and turkeys moving under
the boughs
and we dined by a swamp on bread
and a pomegranate

with stands of canna near us
then poor timber for maybe a mile
of the lowland which
often the river

overflows to the great
loss of those who live there
we lost our way
and that was the day

we found that
tree with the beautiful
good fruit
nameless which I

found never again
it was then
already advanced autumn and the grass
exceeding tall

sand hills along the river
you see
only once whatever
you may say

winter
had passed maybe twelve
times over the wide
river lands

before the son
returned to those regions
when it was spring
and that same tree

was in perfect bloom while
bearing even at that season its
woody apples he said
and the flowers

were of the first order for
beauty and fragrance
very large and white as snow
with a crown or

tassel of
radiant gold stamens
the lower petal cupped
around the others

until it allowed them to unfold
and the edges of all the petals
remaining waved or folded
each flower

set in the bosom of broad leaves
never
the son said did we find
that tree growing

wild anywhere else
so it was fortunate
that he gathered seed and cuttings
and took them

away to bring on
in gardens for
by the time he was fifty
it had vanished from

its own place altogether
only surviving here and there
as a cultivated
foreigner

AFTER DOUGLAS

I could not have believed how my life would stop
all at once and slowly like some leaf in air
and still go on neither turning nor
      falling any more

nor changing even as it must have been
all the while it seemed to be moving
away whatever we called it chiefly
      to have something

to call it as people of the trees call
me Grass Man Grass Man Grass Man having heard that
from me and I neither turn nor am stirred
      but go on

after a sound of big stones to which I
woke as they opened under the hammer
my father and now they always lie open
      with the sound going

out from them everywhere before me like
the bell not yet heard announcing me once
for the one time but not as a name unless
      perhaps as my

name speaks of trees and trees do not know it
standing together with my brothers
and sisters my five senses in all their
      different ages

I see in the eyes of my first birds
where I am coming along this path
in the garden among glass houses
      transparent

walls and now my eyes are perfect finally
I think I must see China but
it is still the New World as I have heard
        there is the mouth

of the wide river that I know as
the Amazon there are tall bitter seas
sharp stones on the ocean the green pelt
        of the northern

continent sinuous to the shore line
and so deep that I reach out my hand to touch it
and feel that I am air moving along
        the black mosses

only now I am in haste no more
anger has vanished like a lantern in daytime
I cannot remember who was carrying it
        but each dried

form that was lost in the wide river is
growing undiscovered here in shadows
the mown rye continues to stand breathless
        in long summer light

gulls flash above sea cliffs albatross
bleats as a goat I see that the lives one by one
are the guides and know me yes and I
        recognize

each life until I come to where I forget
and there I am forgetting the shoes
that I put on and the mountain that I
        have climbed before

there I go on alone without waiting and
my name is forgotten already into
trees and there is McGurney's house that I
    have forgotten

and McGurney telling me of the dug
pits on the mountain and there unchanged
is the forgotten bull standing on whatever
    I had been

CINCHONA

Where that fever itself
hailed from is hid in the original
warming of the unknown
but fever could there be none nor night sweats
numbered agues aestivo-autumnal chills
the conception of evil in the air
until the blood was there to bear them
and where

the blood hailed from the keen
tenor of Anopheles began its
tracery climbing from
water as the blood had done but in time
raising the high note of its inherited
pursuit of a living body within
whose blood to plant a parasite like
a flag

even harder to guess
how the red bark came into its virtues
or for what purposes
of its own it had preserved those magic
properties sovereign against some fever
far in the future restorer
of a blood that for ages would not yet
be there

or how its powers came
first to be known to one who needed them
suffering near the tree
though surely there were stories about that
later which were true to those only for whom
the tree could speak and which made no
sense to those who believed in the words of
Europe

at the age when the flags
carried their hectic over the ocean
westward from Spain from France
from England and the rest and the place was
possessed of them but when the first blood lettings
and convulsions were history
in Peru the wife of the Viceroy
Countess

of Chinchon lay stricken
with that fever of unknown origin
and boundless ambition
that by then seemed endemic everywhere
consuming her daily with its marauding
investiture until she was
merely warm ruins of the woman she
had been

but after so many
in the grip of that delirium had
passed into its homeland
her number completed some long tally
at which point a message for her physician
arrived enclosing red bark ripped
from a tree in those mountains and telling
its use

so when it had given
back her life the tree all at once was seen
as something of value
like gold and with her name it was christened
and though bitter its taste it was sought stripped shipped
to be sold in Spain carried by
missionaries defended fought over
killed for

two centuries and more
before another message this time in
English in Ecuador
found Richard Spruce fresh from the tree's heartland
that fed the Amazon and from his pursuit
there of mosses and liverworts
that still eluded what he thought of as
knowledge

and Spruce with his mouth still
wise to the daily taste of that powdered
bark and his mind tangled
in strands of the long story of seizures
and incursions Columbus cholera the
cross the Countess opened and read
of his commission for the sake of the
empire

British of course to bring
about the transfer from the Cinchona's
flayed and rummaged highlands
of seeds and seedlings of the preferred strains
to be planted in India achieving
thus for England what Hasskarl had
effected recently on Java for
the Dutch

not just what Spruce with his
dubious health and his devotion to
unknown flora rather
than species of a purely economic
importance which when powdered amazing fine
in a chemist's mortar he said
were bereft of almost all their allurement
for him

would have chosen for his
next excursion and he could have mentioned
Hasskarl's own holding back
from an undertaking in which routine
dangers had been compounded by fierce local
jealousy and the officials'
concern for their monopoly of those
raw trees

alerted as they were
to the Dutch scheme so Hasskarl in Peru
calling himself German
signing up with the government there to make
a survey east of the mountains where they hoped
to colonize and there sorting
his seeds and starting them on their furtive
journey

and four years later
Markham trying it for England with his
English gardener his
native boy and two mules the purpose of
his mission discovered his acquaintance with
Peruvian jails his crossing
the Andes alone in winter keeping
ahead

of everyone as it
seemed by then and in that cold fearing for
the lives of the tender
seedlings but at last contriving to get
the frost-bitten survivors to India
where the beds were prepared for them
and they were planted with every care and
soon died

it would be harder for
Spruce he expected and there were besides
wars going on in those
parts and the behavior that wars nourished
and his preparations were scarcely begun
before he was sick again deaf
in left ear unable to walk or sit
without

great pain but he kept on
forming an expedition planning it
still sick when they set out
from Ambato for the mountains where they
would meet the others assemble the rest of
the equipment discover
on reaching the Cinchonas that there were
nowhere

in that plundered region
seedlings remaining so that besides those
hundred thousand seeds he
sorted it seemed to him necessary
to make cuttings and there on the spot contrive
shaded beds to be kept watered
by hand to root them then pack them in earth
they knew

and into baskets for
the muleback journey over the mountains
then into cases on
the raft rigged up for the trip down the rough
river which under heavy rains turned savage
a narrow sluice between snatching
thickets the current at bends smashing them
three times

into the bank with such force
that the cabin collapsed and their pilot
once was swung by a branch
over the roaring water and they could
not reconstruct afterward what they had done
stunned in the sound of the river
to work themselves free into a quiet
passage

opening like a gate
and as the day was ending a place to
put in and begin to
grope through the splintered bodies of trees
that had saved their lives and to feel the cases
of cuttings as though they were touching bones
of their own after a fall and to find
them all

there under the fragile
covers upright and unharmed the small leaves
glowing white while the moon
rose into that night of the dying year
on the river that had become a silence
around them in which they could hear
as they straightened in the moonlight hardly
a word

they said to each other
of all their labors destined in fact to reach
India and once more
be planted and come to nothing and for
a moment there they could not recall what had
driven them all their lives to that
white shore what question what undetermined
fever

INHERITANCE

As many as four thousand
varieties of the opulent pear
it has been said (although
in some languages that number merely
indicates great multitude)
were to be found barely a century
ago treasured and attended somewhere
in fields and gardens of France
that had been cleared of oaks once

and whatever else may have
preferred to grow there the spaces plowed up walled
amended with ashes
dung beans blood and handled with arts passed from
enclosure to enclosure
by a settled careful cunning people
who compared their seedlings and on wild stock
or the common quince grafted
those rare exceptional strains

whose names told no longer this
many a day of lucky otherwise
forgotten Monsieur who
came on this jewel hanging in a hedge
nor of that pharmacist who
in the spring presented his pear blossoms with
feathers plucked from his geese bearing gold dust
he had destined for marriage
with each and waited to taste

their fruit until he obtained
one he thought worthy of his name nothing
of that orchard in which
such a one appeared situated then
at the end of a village

now long since buried in a city nor
recalled one thing of those whose origins
had gone the way of the leaves
and flowers however they

may have been immortalized
each name came to drip all by itself through
the hearing of children its
syllables ripe with anticipation
honeyed and buttered with praise
weighted down with a sensuous longing for
a season overflowing with golden
skins to be cupped in the palm
and one at a time lifted

away so many and so
sweet when their moment came that after it
for all the preserves liqueurs
pies and perries contrived to prolong it
always it was a life lost
and reached for by the abandoned senses
anguished at having failed it again though
juices had run to the elbow
while the next was coveted

for a blush on a tender
cheek and each one was relished for its brief
difference at last there were
simply too many and around the blurred
taste the names of the fruit sank
through the air useless as the drunken wasps
furring with sound the unidentified
remains the late the fallen
bodies so variously

Inheritance

yet so inadequately
known a single kind in one village called
ten different ways none telling
rightly the filling of the hand the rush
of high day to the tongue none
doing more than point in passing among
so many so hopelessly many as
indeed their variety
seemed toward the century's end

to that jury picked no one
remembers how all men and none of them
young to say just how many
kinds of pears should exist in France and when
that was done to place in their
mouths one after the other the proposed
fruit no doubt in sections and thereupon
solemnly chew over each
candidate and vote on it

considering modestly
their ripest deliberations to be
scarcely more than a helpful
preliminary and looking forward
to a day when the tangled
boughs of proliferating nature bent
with its reckless diversity of wild
pears from the Himalayas
to the Straits of Hercules

and the accumulated
riot of human wishes fortune and
art grafted upon them might
be brought within reasonable limits
according to a few clear

standards on a scale of one to ten they
reduced each bite of pear in the darkness
of their mouths and all they could
say of what they held there was

a mumble of numbers through
moustache and napkin meaning whatever
they had agreed the numbers
would mean but the true taste each time slipped from
their tongues undivulged never
to be recalled it made no difference
whether it was blessed with their approval
on its way and elected
to return in its season

for the delectation of
us far in the future or whether it
was relegated to that
blank catalogue compiled from our sweeping
erasures everything they
savored is gone like a candle in a
tunnel and now it was always like this
with our tongues our knowledge and
these simple remaining pears

THE DAY ITSELF

(Harvard Phi Beta Kappa Poem, 1989)

Now that you know
everything does it not come even so
with a breath of surprise the particular
awaited morning in summer
when the leaves that you walked under
since you saw them unfold out of nothing whether
you noticed that or not into

the world you know
have attained the exact weave of shadow
they were to have and the unrepeatable
length of that water which you call
the Charles the whole way to its end
has reached the bridge at last after descending and
gathering its own color through

all that you know
and is slipping under the arches now
while the levelled ground embraced by its famous
facades the ordinary place
where you were uncertain
late moonstruck cold angry able to imagine
you had it all to yourself to

use and to know
without thinking much about it as though
it were the real you suddenly shines before
you transformed into another
person it seems by the presence
of familiar faces all assembled at once
and a crowd of others you do

not really know
rippling in the shimmer of daylight row
upon row sending up a ceaseless leafy
shuffle of voices out of the
current that is rushing over
the field of common chairs one of them opened here
at the moment only for you

and you should know
who that is as the man some time ago
in Greece you remember is supposed to have
said and there was that other of
his countrymen about whom we
are certain of little who was sure already
without having met you that you

could get to know
you whoever that is if you were so
inclined which indeeed you may not have been on
days of uncomfortable dawn
with recognitions bare of their
more proper perspectives and the phrase goes further
to suggest that perhaps you do

not in fact know
you in the first place but might have to go
looking for you when here you are after all
in the skin of the actual
day dressed and on time and you are
sure that you are in the right seat and behind your
own face now is the you that you

wanted to know
is it not and you feel that you have no
age at all but are the same you that you were
as long as you can remember
while every decision that you
made or thought you were making was conducting you
straight to this seat and to what you

would come to know
as today in the middle of which no
other you it seems is present furthermore
what influenced each of your
choices all of the accidents
as they are called and such chances as your parents'
meeting on their own before you

were here to know
where you were coming from those joys with no
histories those crimes painted out those journeys
without names the flawless courses
of all the stars the progression
of the elements were moving in unison
from what you had never seen to

what you now know
you were so long looking forward to no
wonder it floats before you appearing at
once inevitable and not
yet there so that you are unsure
that this time you are awake and will remember
it all assembled to show you

what you must know
by now about knowledge how it also
is a body of questions in apparent
suspension and no different
from the rest of the dream save that
we think we can grasp it and it tends to repeat
itself like the world we wake through

while as you know
it has its limits it belongs to no
one it cannot bring you love or keep you from
catching cold from tomorrow from
loss or waiting it can stand in
its own way so that however you stare you can
not see things about it that you

do in fact know
perfectly well the whole time and can so
loom that you cannot look past it which is more
important you have to acquire
it for yourself but for that you need
gifts and words of others and places set aside
in large part for informing you

until you know
all this which of course may render you no
kinder or more generous since that is not
its function or at least not right
away and may not only make
you no wiser but make it sound wiser to mock
the notion of wisdom since you

have come to know
better and in some cases it can go
to your head and stay there yet we are all here
to speak well of it we treasure
something about it or we say
we do beyond the prospect of making money
and so on with it something you

certainly know
of it that has led to its being so
often compared to the light which you see all
around you at the moment full
of breath and beginnings how well
you know what that is and soon you will start to tell
us and we will listen to you

LIVES OF THE ARTISTS

It was when the school had burned down that he
started making the book
early in the year at the time the moons
of snow were beginning to wane in hollows
out on the plain he had come back to
last year as though it were home bringing
the name they had dressed him in
he was sleeping

in the loft where all of the boys were put
after the fire they slept
up over the horses in the house of
the horses in the horse smell and all night they
heard horses breathing just below their
own breath and hooves in the dark in dry
grass then he began wanting
to make a book

of what he had seen and how it went on
he lay awake hearing
himself want to make pictures the right way
of what was and could not be found ever
again in the day in the steamy
yard of the agency with its panes
of vacant windows rattling
to their own light

a book with no parents since he had none
it would give for the dead
no names but might show some of the same birds
that were called differently in the true place
where he had been small the tails like split
smoke reflected and flights of white shields
and the buffalo would be there
as they appeared

to him the bulls thudding together like
mossy rocks so the ground
shook but how would he make the sound of their
running wake out of the lined pages of
the red ledger where he would draw them
and the rush of their breath as he kept
hearing it his friends would help
who were older

in the time of the buffalo and still
had names from there that you
could draw with a picture Horse-Back Dark Cloud
Black Wolf Hill Man whereas now for himself
how could you draw a Henderson what
was there anywhere that looked like a
Henderson there was only
a word for him

a Henderson in the night who had gone
away in a wagon
to learn to make wagons and who had shouted
"Baldy" with the others and who could read
the new language for the children but
who nursed the tapeworm and was never
content a bad element
always wanting

to go home he would draw friends in the book
with their true hair braided
to the ground before it was cut they would
be talking together in their richest
robes they would be riding off to battle
leading horses they would be singing
he would show the butterfly
of the thunder

on the white horse with birds bringing power
down and the green frog spread
on the dream shield no bullet could pass through
his friends would be chasing the blue soldiers
off the page he would show the ground where
they fought at Adobe Walls the guns
from the houses the hoofprints
going around

and the fight would not be done so his friends
would still be riding in
the open with nothing touching them and
he would still be a boy at home hungry
in summer who had not heard them tell
how it ended how they would fight no
more and none of them would have
been taken yet

far away to the tall fences nowhere
in the south the waiting
nowhere and the days there and the nights there
the strange moon the new hunger they had no
words for and he would have years before
the wagons changed him and he came back
to meet Reverend Haury
who always knew

better and made him a bright Indian
teaching with white words but
in the drawings he would have the dancers
who could dance everything backward they would
dance in the book he would send to Miss
Underwood before his twenty-third
year and his death of causes
no one bothered

to name with so many of them dying
whatever they died of
and then there was only the book and he
had never met Little Finger Nail his
elder by a few years only who
had been herded south to the fences
with the rest of the Cheyennes
when the spiders

had lied to them again and had led them
down nowhere in their turn
but who had seen that he could not live there
and had said it would be better to die
trying to go home and had started
north at night with others of his mind
when the first leaves were turning
he who was their

singer with the Singing Cloud who would be
his wife and her dying
father and the children who had learned to
be quiet and the mothers and the men with
bows and guns knowing that by morning
they must be gone like a summer and
that they were leaving without
the few things in

the world that might protect them the sacred
arrows the sacred hat
and would have only the horizon of
each day to hide in yet he knew they must
not wait for the old power any
longer but must find their own in their
going as his hand often
had drawn out of

nothing the life they could no longer see
the horses flying and
arrows flying and never coming down
the long lances reaching ahead and not
yet touching a thing the war feathers
trailing behind and the dark stars that
were bullets and you could see
by the shields and

what they wore who was there in the fighting
riding into the smoke
of the blue spiders all in a line and
who rode after the spiders to shoot them
off their horses and leave them scattered
on the ground and who took their guns their
coats and bugles he Little
Finger Nail could

make it appear again and again in
pictures and after the
spiders came chasing them to bring them back
and shot at the chief Little Wolf standing
there talking with them and when they shot
a child a girl and in their turn were
driven back fewer and smaller than
they had come he

wanted to make a book of what he had
seen and would see on the
way home so that how they fought and went on
would be there after it was gone but he
must lose more friends to the spiders who
shot them on sight and he must come to
dream of walking in a world
all white before

at a place where one more time they had fought
off the spiders he found
waiting on the ground the book he had been
wishing for with the pages all white blown
open and the sticks of color lying
beside it for him to make into
how he saw them going and
before they crossed

the iron road and the first of the three
wide rivers he had tied
the book to his back with strips of rawhide
around him under his shirt so it was
there as he rode ahead and as he
peered out through bare brush on the low hills
as he circled back to coax
the spiders from

the trail as he fought as he mourned for friends
fallen as the horses
weakened and the first snow fell among them
as they hid without fires as the skin grew
loose over their bones as some crept out
to turn into scouts for the spiders
as the chiefs disagreed and
as they all said

goodbye while the snow fell and they went two
ways it was there as they
crouched in brush huts starving through blizzards and
were betrayed and surrounded and forced to
lay down the fifteen guns they could not
hide and the bows they had made it was
still there as they were herded
into the fort

where Crazy Horse had been murdered after
the promises and as
they were locked in it was there with the few
knives and the other guns they had managed
to hide and through the time of waiting
under guard there he could make parts of
their journey return across
the pages so

little remaining from the whole story
up until then and it
was tied to his back again in the cold
night when they dropped the guards with the first shots
and poured from the windows to the snow
then ran past the walls to the river
keeping together while the
bullets burrowed

into them and the horses came crashing
after them through the drifts
and those who got as far as the river
hid in the bluffs in the hard cold the blood
freezing on their wounds they lay still with
the dead children and women stunned by
loss and when morning whitened
and those who were

living found each other again it was
he Little Finger Nail
who led the last of them out of the ring
of watching spiders into the bitter
white of the hills but there is nothing
in the book except the blank pages
for the rest of it the last
hiding places

the last meat from the snow the last morning
in the hollow above
the empty river and the spiders massed
at the foot of the hill the last loading
of their guns as the roar of rifles
from below rolled toward them and over
the heads of the children and
of Singing Cloud

and the others his voice rose in the last
singing and some joined him
in the death song the men not as many
as twenty *I am going to die now*
if there is anything difficult
if there is anything dangerous
it is mine to do as the
spiders charged to

the breastwork to shoot down into any
still moving and even
then he rushed out at their fire with his knife
raised and they found afterward under his
shirt a book tied with strips of rawhide
to his back and the holes of two Sharps
rifle bullets almost in
the same place through

all its pages it was a colonel who
took it from the body
after what would be called the engagement
an account book stiff with blood and he kept
it for the pictures of which only
one can be seen now lying open
under glass beside other
examples in

the airless hall of the museum red
lines fly from the neck of
the horse on which the man with long braids is
racing and in the white sky are black stars
with black tears running down from them in
the lighted silence through which strangers
pass and some of them pause there
with all they know

PANES

If you get to a place where it happened
you know what you will find in your turn where
so many suddenly once saw the light
for the last time in a rush of sound no
hearing could survive one note swollen by
the whole roar all the shrieks shouts bellows of
the world you will be struck

first probably by how quiet it is
a kind of disappointment waiting for
you like a relative in the common
daylight on leaves and on houses facing
inwards and on the very stones where they
ran flinging up their eyes and fell and where
now you might say there is

nothing to see who were they when they were
there each of them carrying one secret
before they were forgotten as their eyes
drained away their shoes went on without them
their loose bones were dug up to be crumbled
and harrowed into fields and the causes
that had brought them there were

nowhere to be found who were they over
and over until lately their names were
lined in the dust of lists far from their lives
for a while tracks without feet and at last
the light that had directed wheel and fire
for killing found a way to use silver
to make the mirror hold

its image still and retain a picture
of stillness as perfect as that of glass
or silver only with the light reversed
as from the other side of what had once
been daylight so all that had seemed to be
brightest stands out in its open darkness
and it is the shadows

that brim with the stopped light of the moment
never in which nothing will ever move
in which you can see nothing happening
after it has happened and look over
the land where they are lying to the rags
of cloud their uniforms have turned into
the limbs frozen that way

skins of bare night backs of faces yawning
white none of them with names and the numbers
not touching them you can trace the dark wall
to which they had come so soon and the line
of white trees fractured at the wrists splaying
into the darkness which is the sky
for them all as they are

until they are developed and people
suddenly can see them for the first time
only in black and white but even so
among those who are used to such landscapes
in the flesh some say how real the figures
appear to be on their pages and these
go on like the others

peering as though they were hoping to find
a face they knew there or a form they might
have known they keep recognizing something
that is not there and it does not move but
stares without seeing them and continues
to gaze past them when they have turned away
and the book has been closed

never have pictures like those been seen on
paper and the editions multiply
for a while until everyone has had
enough of them and all the backgrounds look
old then it is afterward and the glass
plates are filed in the dark taking up space
with nobody knowing

what to do with them there are so many
and finally they are brought back into
the daylight and arranged in the roofs
of greenhouses so that morning reaches
through those exposed figures to the infant
leaves waiting in rows and draws them upward
as though summer had come

THE WARS IN NEW JERSEY

This is the way we were all brought up now
we imagine and so we all tell
of the same place by saying nothing about it

nobody is ever walking on those black
battlefields and never have we set foot there
awake nor could we find our way across
the unmemorized streams and charred flats
that we roll through canned in a dream of steel
but the campaigns as we know we know
were planned and are still carried out for our sake

with our earnings and so near to us
who sail forward holding up our papers before us
while the towers rising from the ruins and the ruins
the acres of wrecked wheels the sinking
carriers the single limbs yet hanging
from the light fall away as we pass
in whose name it is being accomplished

all in a silence that we are a part of
that includes the casualties the names
the leaves and waters from the beginning
everything that ever lived there
the arguments for each offensive the reasons
and the present racing untouchable
foreground its gray air stitched with wires its lace

of bridges and its piled horizons flickering
between tanks and girders a silence
reaching far out of sight to regions half legend
where the same wars are burning now for us
about which we have just been reading something
when we look out and think no one is there
a silence from which we emerge onto the old

platform only a few minutes late
as though it were another day
in peacetime and we knew why we were there

A SHORT NAP ON THE WAY

In the late
sun of autumn he is sitting alone
by the window the leaves are leaping
high and running beside the train
as though they were playing with a friend
they have grown up with
everything

about him
shows gray the thin face of a professor
administrator executive
the gaunt nose like a fold of paper
the eyes behind the gold-rimmed glitter
of his glasses each
perfect sleeve

of the suit
tailored so it appears to be empty
the silk tie the hands with their silent
pages along whose orderly
rows he is progressing even the
lips motionless as
an old wound

it must be
the sun finding him his eyelids fall shut
his head sinks back and somewhere he sees
colors he knows that come to meet
him slide over him and he does not
have to remember
their faces

to sense what
they are to him and to him only from
the beginning teasing frightening
him seducing him claiming him

through the badlands that are his unseen home
inside the shell of his
head looking

suddenly
childish the patched backs of buildings beside
the tracks flip past facing outward as
though each one were the true facade
they have been forgotten for the new dead
season their panes black
as ditches

by the fields
in October though piled up behind their
veteran weatherboards the brilliant
awnings and bright rags of summer
lie crumpled under dust in the dark where
children ran in for
a moment

to hide and
hearts drummed hands found their way into secret
countries roamed in secret and remain
afterward far off in the light
secret like the spring and summer now at
a small station with
no one on

the platform
two schoolgirls dressed in identical blue
uniforms get off like twins doing
everything together a few
steps away they stop and look around to
the cluttered roofs the
slow flapping

of the old
posters the bricks the streets disappearing
into sunlight this is not yet the
place where they know they are going
this is not the city that is waiting
really for them they
turn to see

each other
in the empty day and they cover their
mouths laughing and run as though something
is chasing them back from nowhere
onto the train where in a while the door
opens to a voice
repeating

a name and
the gray face tips forward into itself
finger bones open the gray briefcase
slip the papers into it lift
from the seat beside it the gray crown of
the narrow brimmed felt
hat that goes

with the rest
sporting one small dark feather far from its
bird he settles it firmly standing
and steps into the aisle and is
gone again taking with him what he wants
and all that he is
forgetting

THE MOMENT OF GREEN

So he had gone home to be shot
he kept telling himself trying
to explain what he was doing
grayed into the backs of shadows
behind walls he thought he had not
seen ever when he was awake
nor those uniforms though they spoke
in blunted fashions the Russian
of his youth the Ukrainian
even of his childhood and they
insisted they knew everything
about him yet went on asking

why he had come home to be shot
which they went on telling him he
seemed to have done and the answer
was something he could no longer
remember now that he was back
where the words had always known him
surely they must know he was not
a spy then what else had brought him
aged thirty five almost half way
around the world after all those
years when he seemed happy enough
to be away first the studies

at the French university
and when they were finished did he
come home he went the other way
out of Europe itself putting
a continent and an ocean
between himself and Malaia
Buromea the rippling grain
around Poltava wind lashing
the plains in winter mounds of beets

tobacco hanging in sunny
doorways the smells of cattleyards
leather and brewing and of parched

wood in the school room where he held
in his mind something of summer
away so far on the other
side of the year and his hand grew
pictures of her he traced the legs
of her grasses lengthening he
followed the lace of her veins to
find where they opened from he drew
the bees in her flowers and on
her leaves the cicada one of
her voices and the grasshopper
part cloud part paper who became

his guide through the dust and winter
and the tissues of days farther
and farther afield ticking through
libraries stations the glitter
of alien cites westward
into trees of strange talk until
he knew the leaves and tenants of
summer to be one as he was
one with the calling that found him
in his time and he followed it
across the Atlantic to its
source as Bates and Wallace had done

sixty years before and he came
as they had done to the river
of rivers moving eastward like
a sea heavy with light and birth
the one-shore river that men from

Europe had christened as it were
after women they had heard of
said to have come from somewhere near
his own homeland they called that flood
the River of Amazons and
he came to the port named by them
for Bethlehem though the bells clanged

from dockside iron and engines
at the railroad terminal more
urgently than from the churches
already old there in the high
days of the rubber bubble when
hour after hour in the harbor
the hulls gave up their marble fresh
from the hills of Carrara for
more boulevards more plazas more
fountains and statues more stately
colonnades public facades so
in the wake of stone cargoes he

went on upriver and beheld
the opera house which the forest
had paid for tall white porticos
designed to be like somewhere else
for a moment and he found work
as a photographer ducking
under the black hood to focus
one instant one face the leaves in
their day one horse running on its
shadow all of them upside-down
as the flash caught them that turned them
gray in the year before the whole

thing fell away as the ships left
the harbors and few replaced them
the docks rotted and grass smothered
railroad sidings and spilled across
marble boulevards the forest
fingered the opera house he heard
day and night the unbroken chant
of summer whirring in ringing
chorus the frogs and toads after
dark each with its chords the high
crickets cicadas grasshoppers
was it to this that they had

summoned him this prompt projected
vision of a bad end under
the lingering forest lightning
this demonstration of what it
amounted to all that human
grasping wringing killing piling
up of vanity that smiling
for the camera and then this
view of the negative with its
black mouth but what could anyone
be expected to learn from it
in the world as it was except

to try something else and he seemed
to be needed in that country
of the grasshopper a post was
waiting for him at Campinas
to work in plant pathology
on studies of insects and their
hosts for the purpose of human
advantage it was the entrance
to the forest to his years of

watching the summer and trying
to write down clearly what he saw
without noticing that it was

his life he was already quite
fluent in the language since he
heard no other and any news
of Russia that reached him did so
in Portuguese some time before
the papers arrived weeks old from
France and the still older letters
in Russian like broken pieces
of dry leaves out of a season
already advanced far beyond
the breathless words and the vanished
time they told of but their frightened

hope their deciduous prescience
rose to him through the familiar
script from those places that were their
trees their country whatever they
might say whatever might happen
where no side by then would believe
what he told them about himself
over his Brazilian passport
why then had he left the summer
to go back and be shot he was
recalling the sounds of long grass
at Malaia Buromea

when he was a child a whisper that
survived only in his mind as
the door opened and they took him
out under guard and down the long
hall to an office with a desk

and above it a head asking
name birthplace what he did for a
living why he had come back to
all the old questions and then asked
whether in fact he had knowledge
of crops their ailments the insects
devouring them the grasshopper

and admitting that they needed
what he knew they set him to work
to save the harvests though it was not
certain whose harvests they would be
or where the home was that he had
thought he would be coming back to
he did not wait for the answers
but this time when he could he made
his way eastward across the whole
of Russia to Mongolia
Manchuria and Korea
Japan the Pacific he had

circled the globe when once more he
saw the molten plain flowing past
the rim of forest and he heard
from the leaves the shimmer of sound
he recognized though he could not
begin to decipher it or
guess who it was intended for
but he heard that it was what he
had to go on listening to
trying to find out how it happened
what it was made of where it had
come from why it continued through

the daze of his return the doors
of his laboratories in
Bahia never again did
he not hear it through the decades
of research and the more than four
hundred published descriptions of
insects and as many of plants
the history of native palms
from the Cretaceous to his own
day it went on after the trees
fell after deaths after learning
after everything had been said

THE RIVER

In the end the crocodiles came into the city

those who had already survived the death of their
civilization

lived in a park
in their eyes there was an iron fence
water near them with tall rushes
like legs of birds
trees overhead some of which they knew
and the crocodiles appeared not to be moving
in the mud

but they had wakened there and they saw the city
appear in flowing shapes and colors that changed
beyond the fence

they held in their eyes the fluttering mouths the teeth
the feet the children the hands
they flowed past as cars
they ascended floor by floor
they roared and disappeared
and seemed to be asleep but never were

inside them on wires conversations raced
like lights moving too fast to be seen
the crocodiles continued as engines and lay still as guns
and were burning even with their eyes closed

at the same time they were admired and were served
and faces came a long way to see them
only one time
and stayed only for a moment

and what the crocodiles
beheld was a dark river never forgotten
never remembered

SO FAR

Less than an inch long and not I suppose
an hour old but taking what must be
the flapping steps of the first morning
into which it has broken its way alone
from the white shell already beyond

recall it spills its spread fingers still
the color of the rainy daylight
across the dark floor I laid myself in other
years and other weather and scrambles
after its head like a kite tail but

not buoyant and the head besides and its
own tail most gray for a gecko a kind
of being which those yellow eyes fixing
me from the floor perhaps have not seen yet
and only from themselves know what they are

attempting while I watch their brown body
of unknown sex and their pale soft limbs making
a floundering lop-sided journey
the only way now for one newly hatched
gecko dragging its right rear leg after it

which leads me to wonder what its chances
can be as it pauses to consider
me with my inches hours definitions
before continuing under the lips
of the square blue pot graven with lines

meant to suggest to my kind a few
leaves of bamboo and in that shadow circling
the sprouting cycad overhead with its
single frond and its ancestry
older than the dinosaurs but now

a species rare if not officially
endangered named for one man Rumphius
who flourished in the Indies a mere three
centuries ago and again the gecko
emerges with its gait like a collapsing

wave under the two-leafed seedling of the lately
discovered species of Pritchardia
that evolved on the crumbling island
of Kauai and I watch the body stumble
out of sight only to sally forth

a moment later with all four of its
hands unfurled and balance in its dance
darker too and decisive and see before it
another hatchling that looks exactly like it
at least to me and now what are the chances

THE PALMS

Each is alone in the world
and on some the flowers
are of one sex only

they stand as though they had no secrets
and one by one the flowers emerge from the sheaths
into the air
where the other flowers are
it happens in silence except for the wind
often it happens in the dark
with the earth carrying the sound of water

most of the flowers themselves are small and green by day
and only a few are fragrant
but in time the fruits are beautiful
and later still their children
whether they are seen or not

many of the fruits are no larger than peas
but some are like brains of black marble
and some have more than one seed inside them
some are full of milk of one taste or another
and on a number of them there is a writing
from long before speech

and the children resemble each other
with the same family preference
for shade when young
in which their colors deepen
and the same family liking for water
and warmth
and each family deals with the wind in its own way
and with the sun and the water

some of the leaves are crystals others are stars
some are bows some are bridges and some
are hands
in a world without hands

they know of each other first from themselves
some are fond of limestone and a few cling to high cliffs
they learn from the splashing water
and the falling water and the wind

much later the elephant
will learn from them
the muscles will learn from their shadows
ears will begin to hear in them
the sound of water
and heads will float like black nutshells
on an unmeasured ocean neither rising nor falling

to be held up at last and named for the sea

IMMORTELLES

Somewhere between the oatmeal
yellow wall with its black marble fireplace
never used
in the house from which the long echoing
flight of steps to the front door
has been gone these many years
and the small red-shingled

done-over farmhouse with its
white trim and driveway furred in blue spruces
where after
a rainy summer alone she looked
up from an empty teacup
one September evening toward
the west where the clouds raced

low over the black waving
trees beyond the dark garden and she stood
up and died
my mother had thrown out those flowers
fashioned of wire and some
kind of beads maybe glass but
in colors such that I

for a long time could not see
that they were flowers balancing over their
black vase that
must never be touched on its island
of lace adrift motionless
on the polished water of
a small table almost

as tall as I was so they
were flowers then and the lines of shell-white
beads circling
in whorls like thumbprints would be petals
while those the shades of unlit
church windows would be leaves but
what mattered about them

as my mother had told me
when I was old enough to understand
was that they
were not real they needed no water
they would never change they would
always be the same as they
were while I stood watching

FIELD MUSHROOMS

I never gave a thought to them at first
with their white heads
cut into slices
under a water of plastic on a blue
section of carpet
or even hanging in a scale
like the piled ruins of a foot

I was shown that when the right time came
you could overturn a dry cow pat
by the edge of a long green swamp
late on a cold
autumn afternoon
as the sun was going down
and there underneath
the real white heads were still growing

I went on finding them
always at evening
coming to recognize a depth
in the shade of oaks and chestnuts
a quickening in the moss year after year
a suggestion of burning
signs of something already there in its own place
a texture of flesh
scarcely born
full of the knowledge of darkness

LUNAR LANDSCAPE

Nobody can tell you
anything new about
moonlight you have seen it
for yourself as many
times as necessary

nobody else ever saw
it as it appeared to you
you have heard all about it
but in the words of others
so that you fell asleep

it was photographed but
somewhere else and without
what was happening inside
its light and whenever it
was rhymed it disappeared

you cannot depend on
it use it for much send
it anywhere sell it
keep it for yourself bring
it back when it has left

and while it is lighting
the ocean like a name while
it is awake in the leaves
you do not need to look at it
to know it is not there

LOOKING UP

How bright the blues are in this latter
summer through which news keeps vanishing
without having appeared but we know
the days as we know the clouds not by name
nor by where they are going the gardens

of the old are like that where every hope
that brought them together is no
more to be seen the stones raised beside
water not after all signifying
length of life but the untouchable

blue place beyond us in which stones are
days as you can see watching the old
at work in their gardens that are never
what they appear to be but already
perfect and transparent as the day is

FOR THE YEAR

for James Baker Hall and Mary Ann Taylor-Hall

If I did not know
I could not tell by
watching the blue sky
with not a cloud
moving across it
in the still morning
above the flying
songs of the thrushes

that in these unseen
hours of clear daylight
one more year even
now is leaving us
one more year one more
decade wherever
it is that they go
once they have been here

and we waited up
for them I stood in
a friend's house high on
a hill looking out
over the city
to the sea ten years
ago and my ears
rang with the midnight

fireworks rising from
the lit streets into
that time with its stars
my hair was still dark
I did not know you
and in the morning
both the puppies barked
and the tiles had come

for the new roof we
are living under
it is already
a year now since we
sat here with friends by
candlelight talking
of childhoods risen
at last from hiding

until we saw that
the candles had burned
past the moment we
had been waiting for
and already it
had slipped through our words
and hands and was gone
and the year was new

without our having
seen how it happened
bringing with it far
from our sight this whole
day wherever it
is going now as
we watch it together
here in the morning

THE REAL WORLD OF
MANUEL CÓRDOVA

And so even
as True Thomas had done
after seven
years had gone
and no cell of his skin
bone blood or brain
was what it had been
the night that the rain
found him alone
neither child nor man
in the forest and at dawn
looking into the swollen
stream toward the sudden
flash of a fish and then

up he saw them
standing around him
more silent than tree shadows from
which they had come
each holding the aim
of a spear for some
moments before they came
without a word and from him
took knife bucket the freedom
of his hands binding them
behind him and hauling him
for days through the green spinning dome
to bring him at last half dead home
into their own dream

in which there was
yet something like time yes
it was still a kind of time as
he turned slowly to realize

where not one of his
syllables touched any surface
and what had been his voice
proved to be nobody's
wondering unheard for days
whether they would eat him as
they kept feeding him dishes
cooked before his eyes
for his mouth alone and across
what felt like his own face

and down over
the meat of him everywhere
first there was the water
they warmed at the fire to pour
on him as a mother
would do and then the knowing finger
of the old man their
leader tracing a signature
of the forest in one color
after another
along him with roots to enter
him and go on growing there
then one night the bitter
juices they held up for

him to swallow while
they watched the apple
climb in his throat and fall
but he thought he could tell
by then a little
of that turning pool
their single will
and if they meant to kill
him there with their sentinel

keeping watch on the hole
in the forest far from the babble
of the village then why was the bowl
passed from his mouth to theirs until
each one in the circle

had drunk and he
looked on as one by one they
lay down and looking on he
discovered that he
was lying down and they
were all together by day
there in their forest where he
understood every word they
were telling him while they
travelled and already
when he came to each tree he
knew that it would be
just where it appeared and they
were its name as they

passed touching
nothing until the morning
when they heard the same birds sing
and he was sitting
with the others in a ring
around the ashes knowing
much of what they were saying
as though it were echoing
across water and he was learning
that they had been dreaming
the same dream then they were filing
like water out of the clearing
and he kept recognizing
the face of each thing

the moment it appeared
also he remembered
here and there the word
to which something answered
them it seemed then that he heard
his own mind and from there onward
through the forest he discovered
how much less he floundered
and crashed while they flickered
with him through the scattered
light their feet in a mastered
music never heard
not even remembered
except as a shared

dream which he found
when they returned
to the village remained
visible around
him a presence that had opened
in the foreground
of the day and as he listened
he could still understand
enough out of the sound
of their words to attend
as the old chief his friend
pointing to the morning summoned
to him the world and
piece by piece explained

where certain medicines
live in hiding where directions
travel in the dark how poisons
wait how the snake listens
how leaves store reflections

which of the demons
are nameless where dying begins
and as the days' lessons
taught him to pronounce
some of the questions
growing in him since
they had him in their hands
he was answered with instructions
from the forest of the old man's

mind carefully
guiding him until he
believed almost that he
had followed his own way
into the only
place alive and when the
moon was right and again they
stood after dark in the empty
tower of trees where one by
one they drank from the bowl and lay
down he thought it was the same day
that he knew but he could see
through each of them an entry
to the forest and as he

turned he went on seeing
everywhere something
the chief was letting
him know even while he was dreaming
what they were all dreaming
together flowing
among the trees entering
cat fur monkey voice owl wing
but he found in the morning
that he was taking

shape in the old man's ruling
dream and was recognizing
in the surrounding
day a forest hiding

from the others
and that his teacher's
whispers and gestures
had rendered his eyes and ears
attuned to powers
haunting plants and waters
that were unknown to theirs
he beheld the ancestors
in his own sleep the bearers
of birth and death the spiders
in charge of night fierce
protectors vipers
of lightning at the fire source
and from the chief's answers

he came to see
that they wanted him to be
the heir of every
secret and therefore ready
to be next on that day
no longer very
distant when their chief would die
for they believed that they
must have somebody
to guide them who already
understood the deadly
aliens steadily
withering their way
into the only

forest somebody who
had been alien and knew
the outer words and how to
turn something of the forest into
what could save them to
trade part of their life for the new
death an outer person who
could teach them how to
have guns yet someone who
had gone with them into
the dream flowing through
the forest and knew
the ancients and the spirits who
never let go

in that way he became
all that the chief taught him
and all that appeared to him each time
he went into the dream
farther and it came
out with him into the day and from
then on was all around him
they gave him a name
and he started to show them
what they could take from
trees that would buy them
guns they gave him
a girl to be with him
they almost trusted him

some of them and under
his guidance they put together
a first cargo or
caravan of rubber
that they would carry for

many days to the river
where he would go to the trader
alone and barter
everything they had brought for
Winchesters and bullets and after
they had brought the guns home to their
roof each of them wore
that night ceremonial attire
feathers claws teeth from their

forest in celebration
and he was given
another girl and then
a third and an old woman
watched over him when
more and more often
after the day's lesson
was done he was taken alone
with the chief at sundown
to the opening in
the trees where the old man
gave him the bowl and began
the chants while on his own
he drank the potion

and the visions rose
out of the darkening voice
out of the night voice the secret voice
the rain voice the root voice
through the chant he saw his
blood in the veins of trees
he appeared in the green of his eyes
he felt the snake that was
his skin and the monkeys
of his hands he saw his faces

in all the leaves and could recognize
those that were poison and those
that could save he was helpless
when bones came to chase

him and they were
his own the fire
of his teeth climbed after
his eyes he could hear
through his night the river
of no color that ended nowhere
echoing in his ear
it was there in the morning under
his breath growing wider
through those days after
the first guns were slung in their
rafters among the other
protectors and the men were
preparing to get more

spending their time doing
what he had taught them working
to change something living
there into something
else far away putting
their minds that far away wanting
guns guns becoming
more ardent still after a raiding
party of enemies sending
arrows out of hiding
near the village had run fleeing
before the pursuing
guns vanishing
leaving one behind dying

and so another caravan
like a snake soon
slipped out in the track of the first one
but the season by then
had moved on and the rain
they seemed to have forgotten
caught them out and began
to drum down
on them all night and in
the misty days as they went on
sliding and splashing in
running mud and then
when they reached the river again
and he took the raft alone

to the trader
the value of rubber
had fallen the rifles cost more
all they had carried bought fewer
bullets he sat down there
that time at table to share
the soup of the invader
and it was a fire
he did not remember
burning over
his tongue to sear
his throat and pour
through him everywhere
melting him so that no water

he drank could cool him and
he wept and imagined
that he would be burned
to death or if he happened
to live would never be sound

in body or whole in mind
again but it lessened
at last and he was left by the bend
of the river with the full count
of guns and bullets on the ground
beside him while the canoe went
back into the flooded end
of the day and without a sound
his companions appeared around

him he watched the weightless
pieces of merchandise
seem one by one to rise
by themselves and nose
their way forward into the trees
then in turn he bent to raise
his load and took his place
among them for the many days'
walking until his surprise
always at a bird-like voice
ahead of him breaking the news
of their return and bird voices
welcoming them with echoes
from their own house

but the old chief was dying
turning before long
into a mummy blackening
in the smoke clouds of the ceiling
and the others were wandering
into themselves hiding
from him exhuming
hatreds that meant nothing
to him they were waiting
he thought for the burying

of the old man and for the mourning
to be done and then they were looking
as he saw for something
from him and the one thing

he had known to show them
was guns a way to get them
a way to depend on them
and now he tried leading them
to the hunt but from
the crash of his gun each time
he fired it the continuum
of calling all around them
fled in echoes away from them
out of range so that it took them
a long time to come
close again and seldom
was it possible to aim
very far through the scrim

of forest and they
with their silent weaponry
went on hunting in the old way
wanting the guns as he
understood then only
for humans such as the enemy
tribes with their angry
language but principally
for the aliens every
change of season so many
more coming up the rivers he
was taken on a winding journey
to see a succession of empty
names in the forest where they

had lived at some time before
the aliens had come with blades for
the white blood of the rubber
trees and guns for whatever
feather or fur or
face they might discover
and in each place he was shown where
the house had stood and men were
shot by the guns and their
women were spread butchered or
dragged off with their children and never
seen again and he learned there were
many voices to avenge but after
each house burned the people had moved farther

into the wild
fabric that they knew and he was told
how at last when the old
chief had led them to the stream curled
like the boa where the field
would be and where they would build
the house that now held
their hammocks and the bundled
corpses creaking in the smoke-filled
ceiling with the cradled
guns among them the chief had called
the place by the name that means world
begins here again or first world
wakens or only world

once more and when they
had led him to every
overgrown scar on the way
of their lives they
went home again to their only

roof where although he
warned them patiently
about the aliens what an army
would be like if it came why
vengeance would never be
final and how they
depended now on the enemy
for guns always they
sat watching silently

for the end of his
words but the voices
that they were hearing even as
he spoke had no peace
for the living and no place
for reason so the restless
passion for guns invaded the days
growing as the gashed trees
dripped and the smoke rose
around the rubber and the cargoes
were shouldered for the wordless
journeys where each time his
exchange with the trader yielded less
for them each time the price

of guns had gone
up and the burden
was lighter than ever on
their way back and when
they had reached the village again
he knew he was alone
and he went out one
time before sundown
into the forest with none
of the girls he had been given

only the old woman
following him and in
the circle of trees stopped to drain
the bowl and he lay down

in the gathering dark watching
for a glimpse of something
the old chief had been hoping
he would come to but was soon beginning
to shiver running
with sweat a nausea clutching
him the coils of writhing
serpents knotting
him on the ground then he was being
shown a sickness like a waving
curtain surrounding
his family and his mother was dying
there and he saw himself lying
with an arrow through him nailing

him down to be walked over
only then did he see once more
the face of the old chief for
the last time standing before
him his protector
and the black jaguar
from the other side of fear
in whose form he could go anywhere
came to him just at the hour
before daylight when from the floor
of the forest curled roots that were
the old woman's hands rose to offer
the bowl that would restore
him and as her face became clear

in the milk of her eye
he saw that she
knew everything that he
had been but as before she
said nothing and after that night he
woke to how far away
was the intangible country
of his ancestors he
began to be
repelled by the frenzy
of their celebrations and they
who so delicately
when hunting could make the
odor of the human body

one with the unwarned
air of the forest around
them now began to offend
him with their ripened
scent they hardly listened
to him or so he imagined
and a silence widened
between them until a band
went on a raid as he found
out later and when the men returned
with eyes ablaze and blood-stained
bodies he learned
only from the shouts that night around
the fire what kind

of game they had taken
that trip what meat they had eaten
and in those days the men
worked without urging and too soon
had another caravan

ready and they set out again
but on this journey storm and rain
would not let them alone
day or night and they thrashed in
mud they were bruised chilled hungry and when
they tried to sleep sitting down
under leaves the water ran
across them as though they were in
a black stream then

with his eyes closed he saw over
and over one fast stretch of river
and each time out on the water
the same familiar
small boat heading upstream near
the white turn where
the current swept out from under
hanging boughs and he looked more
narrowly after
the vessel but never
could see it clearly before
it was gone in the green cover
and he was awake cold and sore
that day they reached the river

built their raft and he
pushed off at break of day
with everything they
had brought and in the misty
dawn poled his way
downstream to tie
up at the trader's landing by
a river boat that he
thought familiar it would be
leaving at about midnight he

heard from the trader as they
loaded a canoe with every
useful thing that he
had been able to buy

except guns
then he took a canoe once
more to where his friends
were waiting for him in dense
forest on the bank he watched their hands
unload the canoe looking for guns
he had brought only this he said the guns
were still on the boat new guns
for shooting through trees the plans
called for unloading them in silence
at midnight to keep those guns
from falling into the hands
of the aliens
he watched their expressions

as he told them he
had to go back with the canoe he
could see that they were uneasy
knew something was wrong so he
pushed off quickly
into the current paddling and by
the time he reached the bend he could see
no one on the bank where they
had been standing only
the trees and then the trader's where he
asked for the remaining tally
of their earnings there and he
withdrew all the gun money
bought clothes for going away

paid for his passage would
eat nothing went on board
feeling numb and cold trying to avoid
their questions lay down and waited
in the dark for midnight with his head
afloat above the floating wood
heard the limbs of wood
from the forest falling into the loud
firebox watched the trees of sparks fade
overhead as the boat started
out into the river his mother was dead
whatever he might need
was somewhere that could not be said
as though it had never existed

ANOTHER PLACE

When years without number
like days of another summer
had turned into air there
once more was a street that had never
forgotten the eyes of its child

not so long by then of course nor
so tall or dark anywhere
with the same store at the corner
sunk deeper into its odor
of bananas and ice cream

still hoarding the sound of roller
skates crossing the cupped board floor
but the sidewalk flagstones were
cemented and the street car
tracks buried under a late

surface and it was all cleaner
as they had said it would be and bare
like the unmoving water
of the windows or a picture
in white beneath the swept sky

of a morning from which the trees were
gone with their shadows and their
time that seemed when we moved there
years before to hold whatever
had existed in the moment

that echoed the notes of our
feet striking almost together
on the hollow wooden front stair
up to the porch and glass door
of the sepia house which once

we were gone would be whited over
we walked with my father
climbing toward his fortieth year
in the clothes of a minister
Presbyterian vacating

a church with a yellow brick spire
on a cliff above a river
with New York on the other shore
by then the Protestants were
moving out of that neighborhood

the building was in disrepair
and a year or two after
he left it the leaking structure
would be sold to the Catholics for
a song and then torn down

and its place would know it no more
remaining empty for
the rest of his life and longer
when he got to the top stair
of the new manse he turned around

to face the photographer
and stood up straight gazing over
the man's shoulder toward the other
side of the street and the square
bell tower the stuccoed walls

stone steps carved frame of the door
rose window that was a wonder
he said of its kind the summer
still floated in the light and before
long he would find someone

with the talent to capture
that sacred architecture
in black and white for the cover
of the bulletin week after
week the name of the church

in Gothic letters under
the noble mass in the picture
and below in slightly smaller
type the name of the pastor
page one inside announcing

every Sunday the order
of service giving the scripture
verses hymn numbers psalter
and text upon which the minister
himself would preach this morning

page two the schedules for choir
practice Christian Endeavor
deacons' elders' and prayer
meetings quiltings clam chowder
get-togethers boy scouts girl scouts

as he gazed he could hear
his own voice circling higher
out of the picture before
him leading them all together
amen amen that would be

the shadowed sanctum where
he would stew in the rancor
of trustees' meetings bicker
over appointments procedure
and money always money

and would watch within a year
his congregation shatter
into angry parties and there
as his own marriage turned sour
disappointed grudging absent

yet his own beyond his doubt or
understanding and the pair
of lovely children who were
also his although never
had he seemed to be able

really to touch them or
address them except in anger
grew up turned from him somewhere
on the far side of their mother
telling him nothing waiting

out his presence dropping their
voices when he would appear
since they had learned to remember
him only as the author
of everything forbidden

he would take to going over
in the evening after
an early supper whenever
nothing was scheduled for
that night and the church stood dark

and hollow to the side door
at the foot of the tower
topcoat flapping and a folder
of papers clutched in the other
hand as he turned the key and

slipped through reaching up for
his hat and pausing to hear
the lock click behind him before
he touched the pearl button once more
to wake to himself the high

green walls lit yellow the air
of a cavern without breath or
sound that had heard no one enter
looming up and the first stair
coughing under his foot

in the wooden night then the floor
of the Sunday School room louder
because there was nobody there
to watch him to hover
above him and wait for him nothing

to be afraid of therefore
the psalmist said we shall fear
not but walk with greater
deliberation pause ponder
rows of chairs closed piano

line of one varnished rafter
to its end while whistling under
the breath over and over four
or five tuneless notes as far
as the closed carved oaken

door of his cold study where
his own blood rose in his ear
like a sea in the dark before
the light spilled down the somber
panelled walls across green

filing cabinets moss under
foot heavy desk all but bare
and behind it the black leather
back of the waiting chair
facing him in which without his

noting it he was aware
repeatedly of another
figure of himself younger
it seemed by maybe a year
or two wearing a shirt

of gleaming white and never
coat over it however
cold the radiator
and the draft at the shoulder
from the black window but that

was the one without error
all along the one with each year
of school completed no favor
to beg nothing to make up for
to excuse or put differently

the one he liked to refer
to as himself and to speak for
when questioned the one he was sure
of the one with the answer
who did not look up and whose

eyes mouth indeed no feature
of whose face he had ever
seen directly but neither
did he glance toward them or
touch the cold chair even

for one moment to sit down there
only patted the desk another
time on his way to the far
door and the organ and choir
stalls the chancel the three

high seats out in the center
where he turned slowly to stare
past the line where the black water
of empty pews came ashore
and to peer up at the arches

that dove into the dark over
narrow bands of faint color
seeping through glass at that hour
he raised his arms facing the farther
wall by way of rehearsal

squeezed his eyes shut to mutter
some benediction or other
and in his Sunday manner
climbed with his handful of paper
into the pulpit to leaf

through his notes and deliver
a passage here and there
his voice returning over
and over to the same threadbare
wandering phrases unfinished

sentences trying with fervor
and sound to kindle from their
frayed ends a redeeming power
whole and irrefutably clear
to the waiting darkness at

last he ran through the entire
sermon as though he could hear
himself from the shadows and after
he had come to the end he stood over
the pages while the echo

sank back from the tones of one more
final word that would sound for
a moment and then lie together
with the others of that year
in a box to be piled

on a shelf and maybe never
opened again before
his last instructions were
carried out and the white pyre
of all his preaching built high

in a garden incinerator
one bright day of another
autumn farther west near
where he had started from but for
the moment the pages lay

still in the unlit core
of the week while the same whisper
of the heedless dark rose closer
to his breath he gathered his paper
together turned out the lights

behind him left by the back door
to the side street and his car
and late haunts a running sore
in his marriage and rumor
soon followed after and took

not long at all to discover
which nicely spoken young helper
had been driving with the preacher
alone at what times and where
how much attention he seemed

to spend on her widowed mother
and sick brother at their
little house around the corner
until he went off to the war
as a chaplain and his

family moved to another
part of town then another
town and none of them ever
came back but the house was still there
somewhere under its dazzling

paint and so was the top stair
where he had turned toward the far
side of the street with the gray tower
the dark ring in the austere
facade and in that place

as when one hand alone for
a moment clinging to air
above the rising water
so quickly is drawn under
that it leaves those who have seen it

asking each other whether
what they have seen was ever
there and they cannot be certain or
as when a face familiar
it seems as the common day

around it with every feature
known and nothing either
lost or surprising may appear
again in its regular
stance and its quiet voice begin

to relay at its leisure
something that the listener
will need to remember
and suddenly the dreamer
is shaken awake so from the low

house with the piled porch furniture
where the old choir director
used to rock in his darkened parlor
and all the way to the corner
instead of the building and its age

there was nothing but the clear
sky of autumn with a barrier
of pine boards sawn raw from their
lives standing along the gutter
around nothing visible

until one came to look over
the edge with the sign Danger
Keep Out and see the latter
mountains the glister of char
on jutting wood the jagged

pieces of remembered color
that had been carried so far
in the dark at last raising their
bright tips out of a glacier
of cinders and fallen sections

of brickwork scorched wallpaper
shreds of its green vine and flower
pattern still waving over
pools of shivering water
and broken tiles from the long red

aisle all heaped up together
naked to the public air
in the smell of wet plaster
and of fire a few days before
and of the leaves in autumn

ONE STORY

Always somewhere in the story
which up until now we thought
was ours whoever it was
that we were being then
had to wander out into
the green towering forest
reaching to the end of
the world and beyond older
than anything whoever
we were being could remember
and find there that it was
no different from the story

anywhere in the forest
and never be able to tell
as long as the story was there
whether the fiery voices
now far ahead now under
foot the eyes staring from
their instant that held the story
as one breath the shadows
offering their spread flowers
and the chill that leapt from its own
turn through the hair of the nape
like a light through a forest

knew the untold story
all along and were waiting
at the right place as the moment
arrived for whoever it was
to be led at last by the wiles
of ignorance through the forest
and come before them face
to face for the first time
recognizing them with

no names and again surviving
seizing something alive
to take home out of the story

but what came out of the forest
was all part of the story
whatever died on the way
or was named but no longer
recognizable even
what vanished out of the story
finally day after day
was becoming the story
so that when there is no more
story that will be our
story when there is no
forest that will be our forest

RAIN TRAVEL

I wake in the dark and remember
it is the morning when I must start
by myself on the journey
I lie listening to the black hour
before dawn and you are
still asleep beside me while
around us the trees full of night lean
hushed in their dream that bears
us up asleep and awake then I hear
drops falling one by one into
the sightless leaves and I
do not know when they began but
all at once there is no sound but rain
and the stream below us roaring
away into the rushing darkness

ON THE BACK OF THE
BOARDING PASS

In the airport by myself I forget
where I am that is the way they are made
over and over at such cost the ripped
halls lengthening through stretches of echoes I
have forgotten what day it is in this light
what time it could be this was the same morning
in which I mislaid the two timepieces
they may turn up again timepieces can be
bought but not the morning the waking
into the wish to stay and the vanishing
constants I keep returning to this was the
morning of mending the fence where the black dog
followed the water in after the last
cloudburst and I kept on trying to tie
a thread around the valley where we live
I was making knots to hold it there in its
place without changing as though this were the waking
this seeming this passage this going through

LAST MORNING AT
PUNTA ARENA

In the first rays the wandering mountain ridge
above the sand plain with its crowd of gray cactus
kindles to peach and orange and a wave
of color burns slowly down the cliffs
these rock faces were born under the sea
but now all we have been and have forgotten
is rising around us from the ash of dawn
into the day that comes to take away
sea birds call across the glassy water
broken shells turn over on the waking shore
another storm perhaps and the ragged
shelter of dry leaves will let in the whole sky
I walk toward it once more following my own
footprints through the new morning and I see
three heads rise just beyond it coyotes
wild dogs they watch me and move off slowly
all the time looking back over their shoulders

MIRAGE

After a point that is passed without being seen
more and more of the going appears to
be going back but that is another
cloud shadow there was never any such
dwelling place although having once gone away
it seems that there must have been a reason
for setting out and then a reason for
thinking so a first season returning
a new ending a being that the hand
reaches for in the dark and finds and goes on
trying to find this time this time the hope
ringing ringing it must all be the sound
of a mind if only because it could
not be anything else floating down once more
over the vast scars of the butchered land
sinking through every ghost that was murdered in
our name the layers of invisible
intentions the word morning in the plural
its fingers of sunlight on floors its trembling
garments its air of promise that large word
its Europe every inch of it turned over
and over by one kind of life burying
and bringing up year after year looking
for another life until at last a single
crow is flying across translucent June pastures
and mustard fields under high tension wires
in rain and between files of pointed trees
on the empty road into the air small children
are running with arms raised toward the clouds
running and falling and I am running
like a small child running with arms raised
falling getting to my feet running on
after all having decided that
I am going to tell the whole story

ON THE OLD WAY

After twelve years and a death
returning in August to see the end of summer
French skies and stacked roofs the same grays
silent train sliding south through the veiled morning
once more the stuccoed walls the sore
pavilions of the suburbs glimpses
of rivers known from other summers leaves
still green with chestnuts forming for their
only fall out of old dark branches and again
the nude hills come back and the sleepless
night travels along through the day as it
once did over and over for this was the way
almost home almost certain that it was
there almost believing that it could be
everything in spite of everything

LEFT OPEN

The shutters are rusted open on the north
kitchen window ivy has grown over
the fastenings the casements are hooked open
in the stone frame high above the river
looking out across the tops of plum trees
tangled on their steep slope branches furred
with green moss gray lichens the plums falling
through them and beyond them the ancient
walnut trees standing each alone on its
own shadow in the plowed red field full
of amber September light after so
long unattended dead boughs still hold
places of old seasons high out of the leaves
under which in the still day the first walnuts
from this last summer are starting to fall
beyond the bare limbs the river looks
motionless like the far clouds that were not
there before and will not be there again

STONE VILLAGE

At the first sight of the old walls the rain
was over it was high summer with tall
grass already white and gold around
the somber brambles waves of them hiding
the house completely from the rutted lane
that ran among brambles and shadows
of walnut trees into the silent village
already it was afternoon and beyond
the barns the broad valley lay in its haze
like a reflection as it does long after
the house has risen dry out of the tide
of brambles and the uncounted sunlight has crossed
the dust of the floors again all the fields
and the shoulders of the stone buildings have
shrunk and the animals have wakened in
the barns and are gone and the children
have come home and are gone and the rain
they say seems to have stopped forever

TURNING

This is the light that I would see again
on the bare stones the puckered fields the roof
this is the light I would long remember
hazed still an afternoon in September
the known voices would be low and feathered
as though crossing water or in the presence
of moment the old walnut trees along
the wall that I wanted to live forever
would have fallen the stone barns would be empty
the stone basins empty the dormers staring
into distances above dry grass and
the wide valley and I would see my own hand
at the door in the sunlight turn the key
and open to the sky at the empty
windows across the room that would still be there

A SUMMER NIGHT

Years later the cloud brightens in the east
the moon rises out of the long evening
just past midsummer of a cold year
the smell of roses waves through the stone room
open to the north and its sleeping valley
gnarled limbs of walnut trees and brows of extinct
barns blacken against the rising silver of night
so long I have known this that it seems to me
to be mine it has been gone for so long
that I think I have carried it with me
without knowing it was there in the daytime
through talk and in the light of eyes and travelling
in windows it has been there the whole way
on the other side like a face known from
another time from before and afterwards
constantly rising and about to appear

AFTER THE SPRING

The first hay is in and all at once
in the silent evening summer has come
knowing the place wholly the green skin
of its hidden slopes where the shadows will
never reach so far again and a few
gray hairs motionless high in the late
sunlight tell of rain before morning
and of finding the daybreak under green
water with no shadows but all still the same
still known still the known faces of summer
faces of water turning into themselves
changing without a word into themselves

NOTES

PAGE *3*   *The Blind Seer of Ambon.* Georg Eberhard Rumpf, 1627–1702, more usually known as Rumphius, lived most of his life in the Dutch East Indies and was the author of *The Ambonese Herbal.* See *The Poison Tree*, E. M. Beekman editor and translator, University of Massachusetts Press, 1981.

PAGE *5*   The most complete work on Marin so far is *Don Francisco de Paula Marin* by Ross Gast and Agnes C. Conrad, University Press of Hawaii, Hawaiian Historical Society, 1973.

PAGE *41*   *After Douglas.* David Douglas, 1799–1834, Scottish naturalist for whom the Douglas Fir is named, fell into a bull trap on Mauna Kea, Hawaii, and was killed by a trapped bull. Douglas's North American Journals, and a critical memoir by John Davies, were published under the title *Douglas of the Forests*, University of Washington Press, Seattle, Washington, 1980.

PAGE *59*   The biographical account of *Frank Henderson* by Karen Daniels Petersen was published with facsimiles of Henderson's book of drawings by the Alexander Gallery and Morning Star Gallery, in a volume entitled *American Pictograph Images: Historical Works on Paper by the Plains Indians*, New York, 1988. Little Finger Nail's story is based principally on material in Mari Sandoz's *Cheyenne Autumn*. Hastings House, New York, 1953 (and subsequent Avon paperback).

PAGE *76*   *The Moment of Green.* The protagonist is Gregorio Gregorievich Bondar, 1881–1959. Born in Poltava, Russia. Author of many botanical and agricultural studies including *Palmeiras do Brasil.*

PAGE *96*   *The Real World of Manuel Córdova.* Acknowledgment is given for the permission granted by F. Bruce Lamb, author of the book *Wizard of the Upper Amazon*, published in 1987 by North Atlantic Books, Berkeley, California, which provided the historical basis for the poem.

A NOTE ABOUT THE AUTHOR

W. S. Merwin was born in New York City in 1927 and grew up in Union City, New Jersey, and in Scranton, Pennsylvania. From 1949 to 1951 he worked as a tutor in France, Portugal, and Majorca. After that, for several years he made the greater part of his living by translating from French, Spanish, Latin, and Portuguese. In addition to poetry, he has written articles, chiefly for *The Nation*, and radio scripts for the BBC. He has lived in Spain, England, France, Mexico, and Hawaii, as well as New York City. His books of poetry are *A Mask for Janus* (1952), *The Dancing Bears* (1954), *Green with Beasts* (1956), *The Drunk in the Furnace* (1960), *The Moving Target* (1963), *The Lice* (1967), *The Carrier of Ladders* (1970), for which he was awarded the Pulitzer Prize, *Writings to an Unfinished Accompaniment* (1973), *The Compass Flower* (1977), *Opening the Hand* (1983), and *The Rain in the Trees* (1988). His translations include *The Poem of the Cid* (1959), *Spanish Ballads* (1961), *The Satires of Persius* (1960), *Lazarillo de Tormes* (1962), *The Song of Roland* (1963), *Selected Translations 1948–1968* (1968), for which he won the PEN Translation Prize for 1968, *Transparence of the World*, a translation of his selection of poems by Jean Follain (1969), *Osip Mandelstam, Selected Poems* (with Clarence Brown) (1974), *Selected Translations 1968–1978*, *Iphigeneia at Aulis* of Euripides, with George Dimock, Jr. (1978), *Vertical Poetry*, a selection of poems by Roberto Juarroz (1988) and *Sun at Midnight*, a selection of poems by Musō Soseki, translated with Sōiku Shigematsu (1989). He has also published four books of prose, *The Miner's Pale Children* (1970), *Houses and Travellers* (1977), *Unframed Originals* (1982), and *The Lost Upland* (1992). He has been a recipient of several fellowships, including Rockefeller, Guggenheim, Rabinowitz, NEA, Chapelbrook grants, and awards including the Bollingen, the Harriet Monroe, Shelley, Maurice English, Oscar Williams and Gene Derwood, and Aiken-Taylor prizes for poetry. In 1974 he was awarded the Fellowship of the Academy of American Poets. In 1987 he received the Governor's Award for Literature of the state of Hawaii.

A NOTE ON THE TYPE

This book was set on the Linotype in Janson, a recutting made direct from type cast from matrices long thought to have been made by the Dutchman Anton Janson, who was a practicing type founder in Leipzig during the years 1668–1687. However, it has been conclusively demonstrated that these types are actually the work of Nicholas Kis (1650–1702), a Hungarian, who most probably learned his trade from the master Dutch type founder Dirk Voskens. The type is an excellent example of the influential and sturdy Dutch types that prevailed in England up to the time William Caslon (1692–1766) developed his own incomparable designs from them.

Composition and printing by Heritage Printers, Inc.
Charlotte, North Carolina
Bound by Kingsport Press, Inc.
Kingsport, Tennessee
Designed by Harry Ford